piano music repertoires

SHIN-ICHIRO IKEBE

"Sway Green Treetops"
for Piano

池辺 晋一郎

《ゆさぶれ 青い梢を》
ピアノのために

zen-on music

「ゆさぶれ　青い梢を」は、第8回浜松国際ピアノコンクールの委嘱により、2012年11月15日から17日にかけて行われる同コンクール第2次予選の課題曲として、作曲された。

演奏時間：約6分30秒

SWAY GREEN TREETOPS was commissioned by the 8th Hamamatsu International Piano Competition. It was composed as an obligatory work for the second stage of the Competition, held on November 15, 16 and 17, 2012 in Hamamatsu.

Duration: approximately 6 minutes 30 seconds

SWAY GREEN TREETOPS for Piano

The title derives from the beginning of a poem, *Wakareru Hiru Ni (At noon when we part)* which is included in *Wasuregusa Ni Yosu (To the day lily, 1937)*, a poetry book of Michizo Tachihara (1914- 39). I absolutely love his works and I can recite almost all of them.
The poem consists of fourteen lines and begins as follows.

Yusabure Aoi Kozue wo (Sway green treetops).
Mogitore Aoi Konomi wo (Pick green fruit).

I didn't intend to transform the poem into my composition, but Michizo's words evoked the music. Even so, repetition of ascending figurations may represent my image in which I look up at treetops. I strongly hope that performer's poetic fancy will open a variety of musical world.

Shin-ichiro IKEBE

NOTE
I kept pedaling indications to a minimum. At points without any indications, pianists should choose between sustain, sostenuto and soft pedals by themselves. I hope it makes diverse and individual expressions on the performance.

ゆさぶれ　青い梢を　　ピアノのために

タイトルは、僕がそのほとんどの作を諳んじているほど溺愛する詩人・立原道造（1914〜39）の「わかれる昼に」（詩集「萱草に寄す」1937年）の冒頭。

ゆさぶれ　青い梢を
もぎとれ　青い木の実を

と始まる全14行。だが、この詩を音楽に置換させたつもりはない。道造の詩が曲想を呼びさましたのである。とはいえ、上昇にこだわるフィギュレイションは、梢を見上げる作曲者の心の具現ではあっただろう。演奏者の詩的感興により、さまざまな音世界が広がることを、強く望んだ。

池辺晋一郎

NOTE
Pedalingの指定は必要最小限にとどめている。指定のない箇所は、Sustain、Sostenuto、SoftすべてのPedalingを、演奏者自身に考えてほしい。そのことにより、この曲の演奏に関して、多様性と個性が表出されることを、作曲者として望んでいる。

SWAY GREEN TREETOPS

for Piano

Shin-ichiro IKEBE

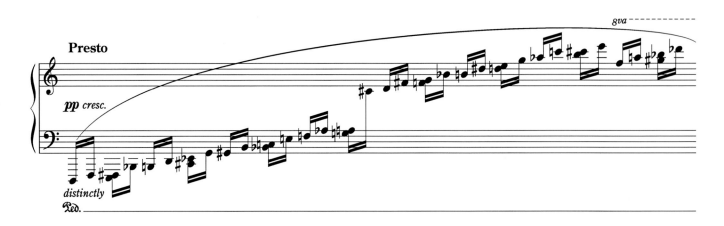

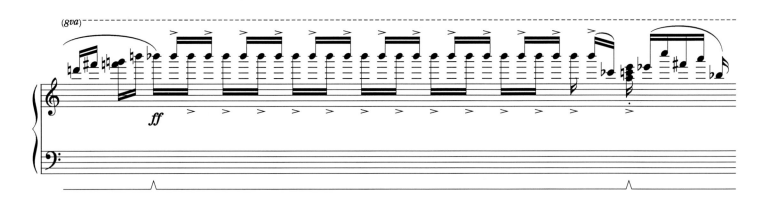

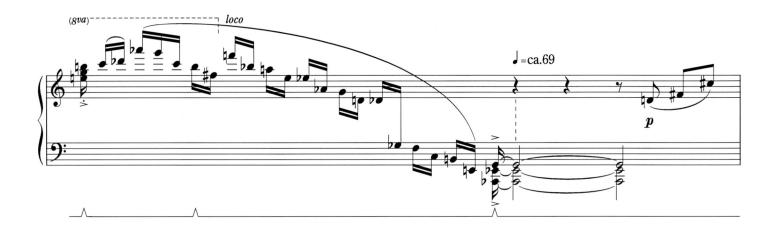

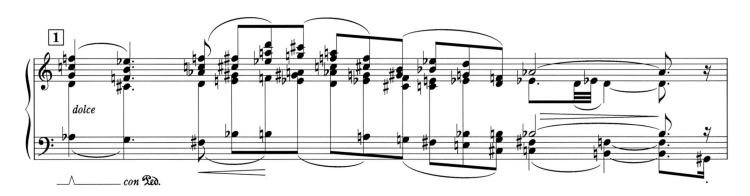

10

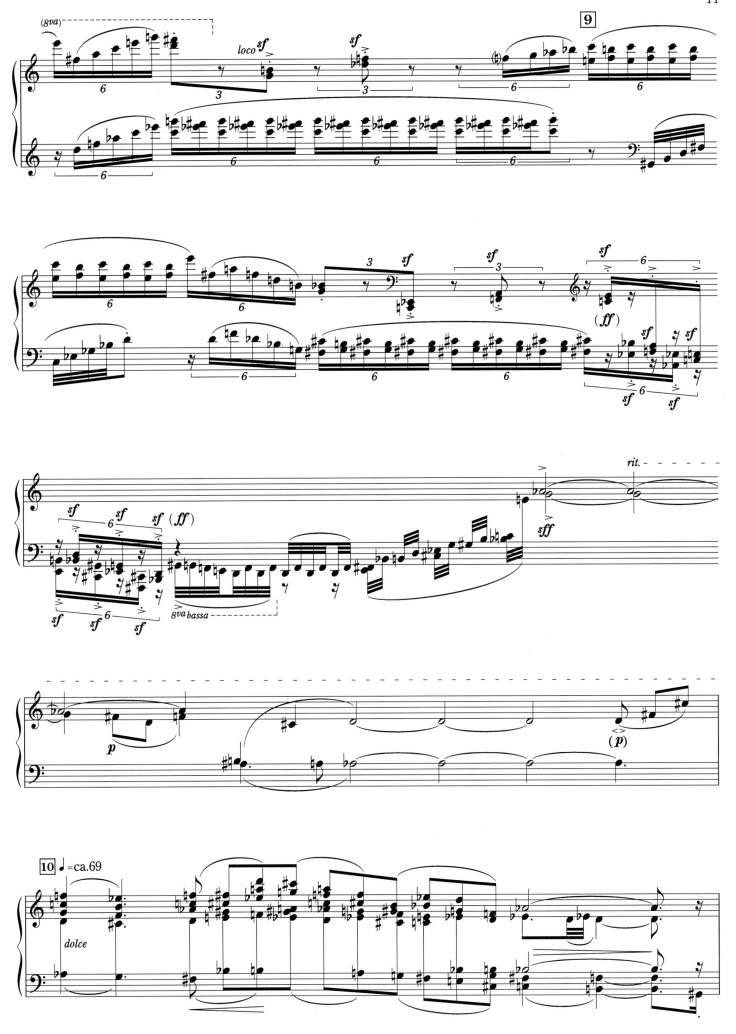

池辺晋一郎：ゆさぶれ　青い梢を　　　　●

作曲————————————————————————————池辺晋一郎
第1版第1刷発行————————————————————2012年4月15日
第1版第2刷発行————————————————————2012年11月15日
発行————————————————————————株式会社全音楽譜出版社
————————————————————東京都新宿区上落合2丁目13番3号 〒161-0034
————————————————————————TEL・営業部 03・3227-6270
————————————————————————————————出版部 03・3227-6280
————————————————————URL　http://www.zen-on.co.jp/
————————————————————ISBN978-4-11-169018-3

複写・複製・転載等厳禁　Printed in Japan

1211003